21 DAYS

LISA L. GILLIAM
TRACY M. WORLEY

COPYRIGHT

Paperback ISBN: 978-1-957751-15-3

Ebook ISBN: 978-1-957751-16-0

Edited by: Nicole Evans

First paperback edition, 2022

JOURNAL JOY

An *Imprint* of Journal Joy *Publishers*

www.thejournaljoy.com

DEDICATION

This book is dedicated to all who are on a journey to healing and self-discovery. We each have a story to tell so have the courage to share your story if you so choose. Should you decide to share, stay the course despite the opinions and judgements of others. Be resilient in your quest to achieve complete healing and have the determination to get back up if you fall. Trust the process, have faith and keep moving forward. No matter what, don't give up!

Dedicated in memory of my parents Leonard (Jr.) and Dorothy Gilliam. You both are loved and missed!

Dedicated to the loving memory of my Daddy, Gordon Worley, Jr. - Boppy

Are you ready to self-reflect, move ahead, and live well through your relationship matters?

Lisa L. Gilliam and Tracy M. Worley offer transparent, yet faith inspired guidance on how to accomplish this in their book *21 Days*. These friends who met at Calvin Coolidge High School in Washington, DC more than 30 years ago creatively and candidly share their personal past connections and encounters, as they introduce their literal 21 Days No Contact Challenge, which assists with collaborative, pensive consideration and progression towards healthier dating and interrelations. *21 Days* is a cognizant approach helping readers understand Lisa and Tracy's journeys, while hopefully showing a way for them to be mindful of their own interactions.

Get set to take a path down an accessible avenue toward better companionship and relationship triumph. A no nonsense yet expressive guide with questions and plenty for you to consider. Enjoy!

Contents

DISCLAIMER

This Work is written by Lisa and Tracy, the referenced blog post, poems, and song lyrics are and continue to be owned solely by Lisa Louise Gilliam. The prayer written in the Work is and will continue to be owned solely by Tracy M. Worley.

All Scriptures referenced are from the Holy Bible, King James Version

- **Who Is The Real Me?** Songs and Lyrics written by Lisa Louise Gilliam Volume 3 PAu3-068-432 © October 13, 2006 Additions have been made to this Work since copyright.

- **How Do You Know?** Songs and Lyrics written by Lisa Louise Gilliam Volume 3 PAu3-068-432 © October 13, 2006

- **About Slow Cooker** Songs and Lyrics written by Lisa Louise Gilliam Volume 4 PAu3-619-483 ©May 24, 2012. The title has been changed for the purpose of this Work.

- **I Give Up On Us** Songs and Lyrics written by Lisa Louise Gilliam Volume 4 PAu3-619-483 © May 24, 2012

- **Shining Star**-Songs and Lyrics written by Lisa Louise Gilliam Volume 4 PAu3-619-483 © May 24, 2012

- **Graphic Visionary Poem** originally written by Lisa Louise Gilliam March 13, 2014. The title has been changed for the purpose of this Work.

- **Proceed with Caution...Maintenance is Necessary!** Originally written by Lisa Louise Gilliam March 11, 2011, for a Blogger Blog Post. Recent additions have been made for the purpose of this Work. This blog no longer exists.

I, Lisa, have always been fascinated by all types of relationships. Although many of my relationships were more reason and season, rather than lifetime relationships, I learned some very interesting lessons from each one, whether it was a familial, significant other, friendship, or situation ship. Those who know me know that I have a Master's Degree in Education and Human Development with a major in Community Counseling from The George Washington University (GW) and twenty years of experience as a counselor and educator. However, what you may not be aware of is that in 2004 I applied and was accepted to Nova Southeastern University (NSU) in Davie, Florida, to earn my Ph.D. in Conflict Analysis and Resolution. I didn't want to use that degree in the manner of most. I wanted to use my Ph.D. degree to encourage and empower individuals and couples contemplating marriage to build a healthy foundation based on effective communication. It's my opinion that having a healthy foundation can help to create successful relationships and reduce conflicts. However, I also believe we are a product of our environment(s) or our past unless we decide to change. I wanted to change. In addition, I wanted to help others change and mend broken relationships of all types.

You may be asking why study Conflict Analysis and Resolution instead of becoming a marriage and family therapist? Well, my answer to this question is simple. After counseling so many people, I began to realize that conflict appeared to be a common denominator for many of the clients I've seen. More often than not, it was a conflict within the individual (inner conflict) and no direction of how to resolve it. On the other hand, for those who were dealing with a conflict with someone else (interpersonal conflict) they didn't have a desire to confront the other person(s) and resolve the conflict. All of these conflicts seemed to cause even more problems when the individuals were interacting in any kind of relationship, especially romantic relationships.

I have heard some say that the lack of understanding is what leads to failed relationships, I don't completely agree. During my counseling sessions, I learned firsthand that one of the major reasons for many failed relationships is the lack of communication. In order to understand what is being said, you have to be able to speak and listen. This lack of communication is often started as a result of conflict, and without a solid foundation it can become difficult to build any relationship. For this reason, I believe effective communication is essential long before understanding ever comes into play.

The year I started my Doctoral Program I had death in my family. I wasn't as focused as I needed to be. The costs associated with the doctoral degree prohibited me from completing it at that time. This never changed my desire to help others reduce conflicts and provide conflict resolution skills. Time went on, and I continued to counsel couples both married and single, as well as teach parents parenting skills. Moreover, a lot of my counseling career was spent working with youth individually or with their parents and/or families. I also counseled adults individually. I have always considered counseling a give and take relationship so to speak. I have never been married. I don't have children and yet I've been able to help many people resolve conflict and communicate in a healthier manner over the years. So although I helped my clients work through their conflicts, I also learned a lot from them to help me work through my own interpersonal and other conflicts.

Who Is The Real Me? written by Lisa Louise Gilliam

I am giving and caring but when expressing the trials, I have experienced in my life or my pain, I am often misunderstood. People say that they know me, but they really don't know me at all. I have lived out of bags, bins, and boxes for the majority of my life. By age 33, I had moved over 20 times. I had baggage!

I had been in what seemed to be an unsolvable situation in that I had been unemployed off and on for years. How could this be when I have a master's degree and taken doctoral classes? I am educated, but my education left me with more than $120,000 in student loans to repay and to date, no full-time job that has paid me a salary of at least half of what I owe.

Therefore, being in this situation there were times when I would have to fight off depression and suicidal thoughts as Satan tried to stimulate my mind to think things that were contrary to my purpose and why God created me. I came face to face with the reality that the poem I wrote in the past, "No More Thoughts of Suicide", were not thoughts of my past, but thoughts I was still dealing with in the present. My life was in a downward spiral, and I became saddened that once again I had succumbed to the depressive thoughts of my situation. The little bit of self-esteem I had left seemed to dwindle away along with all my self-worth.

Due to the sexual abuse, molestation and rape that occurred in my life I often got involved with the "wrong" man and found myself in unhealthy relationships or as we call them now, "situation ships". This led to an array of often inappropriate sexual thoughts that tended to penetrate my mind mentally, stimulate me physically, and tried to lead me down a path of destruction spiritually, so even though I was trying to live in the present, my past was so real. If I were quiet for any length of time, I could often hear my past calling my name.

Thus, to drown out the voices of my past, I would have to press on and seek the Lord in prayer for encouragement. I know I did not do this nearly as much as I should have, yet I would do my best to stay focused, praying that I would eventually achieve God's purpose and will for my life.

Meanwhile, I turned to food as a vice and I would savor and seek excessive starches and sweets, which as a diabetic, diagnosed in September 2003, could negate my very existence if my blood sugars were not controlled and they were not controlled for years. Moreover, I would tell myself I was an emotional eater because that sounded much better than saying I was a glutton, but in reality, the two are very similar and I could fit in either category.

The truth is I held on to the familiar things of my past, hoping for a brighter future that sometimes I never really expected to come. Isn't that dumb? Intellectually, I know, but oftentimes my emotions dictated otherwise. I guess too many of my wounds never fully healed and the scars from the bruises and the pain from removing the bandage at times was too hard for me to allow change to take place. Change in my belief about who and what I am. Knowledge may be power, but it requires action to change.

It's obvious that I have not moved on from all my past pain because after speaking to some people something inside of me would change, anger would arise, and I would explode! I would then find myself bringing up past arguments and pain that I felt others caused which simply meant I had not truly forgiven them, did not want to forgive them or just hadn't healed yet. Now I believe that no one else can cause me to feel anything. My feelings, my actions, my thoughts, my words are just that-mine, and I am the only one who can control them. Who knows? Maybe I lashed out because at times I felt I was not good enough to receive anything positive from others, including love. Maybe I became depressed when I started keeping my deepest thoughts to myself because I got tired of my "friends" saying, "You're so negative" or ``You're draining me!" Maybe my knowledge about who I was had not caught up with the woman I was destined to become.

Contrary to popular belief, I don't have or know every answer although I usually have a response for everything. Really, I am human, just like you. In some areas of my life, I need healing too! This was not good, but true. It is not a "cop-out" or an excuse but when I first wrote this poem, it was my reality.

So, I am asking you, please don't hate or judge me because you can't understand why with all the gifts and talents God has given me, there are still parts of me that I don't love. I realize that sometimes healing is a process. I am on the journey of becoming whole in my life and I believe eventually I will achieve change-mentally, physically, spiritually, and financially but maybe not in the order it is listed.

This is who I am. I mean who I was because with God's help, safely, swiftly, and successfully, my head is being lifted. I am finally "facing me" and taking charge of my emotions and doing the work I need to do to begin to walk on the straight and narrow path...again. Ultimately after I finished sulking in what I thought was my reality, I remembered that I wake up with brand new mercies daily. Therefore, I thank God for His grace, which is sufficient for me. My self-worth is valuable, and my self-esteem has increased. I am loved and I am now moving forward from my past to the present-The Real Me!

I wrote this poem years ago, always believing that God would work out every negative situation in my life. Even when I have sinned, and oh boy have I sinned, He has proven himself to be a forgiving and loving Father time and time again. I know I would be nothing without Him.

As you read this book you will find out about various events that have taken place in my life. I realize that the information I share may be hurtful to those who read it and have had a front row seat in my life. I do want to apologize in advance to anyone who may be negatively triggered, but I no longer want to be silent about the trauma that I have endured since I was a child. Thus, I am writing this book not to harm you, but to free myself. Contrary to popular belief, it has not always been easy for me to tell my story especially because although some terrible things have been done to me, I too, have done some horrible things in my life that I am not pleased about. However, since I have been sharing parts of my story in public for a while now it has become easier to do. I do not like for people to find themselves hurting and if talking about my life and telling my story will help others avoid some of the pitfalls that I have experienced, it is well worth it. The events I speak about in this book are not in chronological order especially since there is a lot of crossovers with my experiences. I have experienced so much trauma and death over the years-actual physical death as well as death or loss of relationships, abandonment, rejection, and pain that honestly there were several times I felt like I was on a roller coaster, especially with regards to my relationships.

Have you ever been on a roller coaster? What made you want to ride it? Did you watch the roller coaster from afar? Did you see how there was a slow beginning, twists and turns, upside down spins? Did you still want to ride it? Sure, you did, if you like roller coasters like I did as a child, I was game for an adventure! I knew it was a slow beginning, but I also anticipated the thrills I would experience while riding the roller coaster. I knew as soon as I reached the top I would drop at a rapid speed and have many twists and turns along the way and may even feel like the coaster would fall off track but yet, I would still ride! Then what happened, I began screaming my lungs out in fear, but I was still securely fastened in my seat. I believed that no matter what, I would reach the final destination (the end of the ride) safely. I am not sure about you but sometimes I had to mentally prepare myself first before I was ready to get on the ride. Well, the roller coaster is symbolic of my life! I have had some slow times. I have also had some things happen at a rapid and thrilling pace. Then there were also some twists and turns. I often felt like my entire life would fall off the track, but God still secured me in His arms and protected me from death. I praise God for never leaving or forsaking me… whether I deserved it or not!

Notwithstanding, there have been times it has been difficult for me to trust God completely in every aspect of my life. I like roller coasters, but I don't always like what my body goes through while I am on them. I feel the same way about my mental, physical, and spiritual life. I must remind myself that the same One (God) that kept me safe while I was on the actual roller coaster ride, keeps me safe on my roller coaster ride of life, daily. Since this roller coaster of life includes my relationships, I believe that one day, I will no longer make the poor choices and decisions I have made in the past, and that God will continue to keep me safe and sane as I continue to "do the work" necessary through prayer and counseling.

My roller coaster ride of life had me thinking. Could it be all the experiences of my past played a role in my broken relationships to date? I think so. I feel like my past experiences from being sexually abused and molested as a child, and then raped during my freshman year in college played a huge role in the way I treated myself and how I allowed others to treat me in relationships. A year after the rape I found myself turning to sex to fill the voids I was having in my life. As a Christian, I was taught that engaging in sex outside of marriage was wrong but at the same time it provided me comfort and a way of escape from the trauma I had experienced.

In turn this created another interpersonal conflict. Moreover, even when I didn't want to engage in sex sometimes, I did because I didn't want to be raped again. I often didn't make wise decisions. Therefore, I must give credit to God for giving me the knowledge, wisdom, skills, and abilities to counsel so many people who had also experienced trauma and conflict, especially since I did not become aware of the horrible patterns that had taken place in my life until recent years.

I realize now that I could not change what I did not know. I also discovered that I was not alone. I spoke to so many of my female friends who found themselves loving the "wrong" person and some even marrying the "wrong" person, becoming friends with individuals who did not mean us well. Too many times the guy that my friends thought they would get in a relationship with or marry somehow ended up being a friend with benefits or situation ship. My friends became the one who caught feelings while the men they loved moved on to their next relationship which often ended in marriage. For some, that same man that left them for someone else, still wanted them to remain in their lives. Go figure! Sad to say, that was the case. The men simply wanted their cake and eat it too. Since the women's self-esteem and self-worth was not at the level that it should have been, that type of behavior was allowed instead of being dismissed. As a result, they were heartbroken and sometimes bitter and angry.

I could identify with this because there were times that I would get involved with guys hoping that at least my love life could prosper in a healthy direction, but that was usually not what happened. It is crazy to think that I have been able to counsel so many couples, marriages, parents, and families over the years but was not able to be in a healthy relationship myself. Well, after counseling others who had been brokenhearted, listening to my friend's stories, and almost 20 years of off and on-again relationships of my own, I was finally ready for a change. I wanted to heal and find love and joy in my life again! I knew a few other friends who had experienced similar situations.

God laid it on my heart to start the 21 Days No Contact Challenge, inviting them to join me. Thus, I contacted three of my friends and told them about the God-inspired idea. I believe that God hand-picked each of us to participate in the challenge. The other ladies never met, but I knew each of their stories. I thought we could all benefit from this process together. They say it takes 21 days to form a new habit, but we found out it might take much longer to separate our hearts from our heads! We were getting ready to embark on a journey that created a new (positive) habit and changed our lives forever. A journey that showed us if we truly wanted to change the outcomes of our relationships, we had to raise our self-esteem and self-worth. This meant we had some work to do! We were valuable but had not acted as such!

First, I (Lisa), set some ground rules and made sure that each person was comfortable with sharing their contact information with the other ladies. Next, I set a time when everyone could call daily via video chat at 6:30am. I decided to use Google Meet to meet with the ladies every morning for the 21 days. We couldn't have any contact with those that we were trying to move forward from unless certain stipulations were stated at the beginning on the first day of the meeting. One of us had been seeing someone who had recently been diagnosed with a health issue and he was supposed to call to keep them abreast of the situation. Funny thing is during this intentional 21-day hiatus, he did not call or text, so there was no update on if he was doing well or not. Another person in the group had an unsettled business matter, so if he contacted her about that, it was the only exception to speak to him, since he was a major reason for her joining this process.

Other than those two situations, there was to be no contact period! This included video apps, text messages, phone calls and emails. We also had to block the individuals on our phones (including social media if you were not strong enough not to look at the man's social media page during the 21 days). Furthermore, for the duration of the challenge, if the man contacted us, we could not respond other than for the 2 stipulations mentioned previously. The other rule was that we could not give the men any warning about what we were doing. 3 of us followed this rule and 1 did not.

There was one caveat in this process, if we had contact with the person in any form or fashion, we would have to start day one all over again. Who wants to do that? Not me! 2 of us had contact with their individuals by text and phone call so they had to start over again the next day. At least it was only one day in, and not several days. For the 2 ladies who contacted the men they were dating, their last day was the day after the date we were scheduled to end, so they basically ended up with a 22-day challenge instead of 21 days. An exception was made when one of the ladies had additional contact with the man they were dating halfway through the process. The ladies met as a group and decided to not have her start over since the contact was made due to medical need.

Each person had to find a therapist and attend at least 1 therapy session during this process. Three of the four attended at least 1 session. One of the ladies contacted someone but was placed on a waiting list. One of us had previously scheduled weekly sessions with their therapist for the month prior to knowing that the 21 Days No Contact Challenge would be established. One lady found a counselor and started her session but had to change counselors due to insurance and another lady scheduled her session with a therapist she had already seen. We also could not tell anyone about the process other than saying we were in a daily prayer group. Any additional details could not be revealed to anyone else other than our therapists.

It was made clear that therapy should continue if the therapist and individual believed it was needed. Very rarely, if at all, is 1 therapy session enough to unpack a lifetime full of issues, concerns, conflict, and trauma.

A vital step in this process was writing down our thoughts, our feelings and the growth or lesson we learned each day prior to the prayer meeting via video chat. The reason for this is because people often intertwine their thoughts with their feelings, but they are 2 separate entities. Each morning during the video call, we shared our journal entries. I instructed the ladies to write down the "wins" (seemingly small accomplishments) so that when the losses came (anytime we failed or had a bad day related to how we felt about our significant others) we could reflect upon the times when we were victorious. After sharing our journal entries, each lady would have an opportunity to comment on what was shared and if we so choose, give feedback, and speak about how we could make better decisions and choices. Although we started this challenge because we no longer wanted to desire the men who had hurt us, we were clear that we were doing this for ourselves. Before each call ended, someone led us in prayer. Sometimes we would check on each other during the day via text and forward Instagram messages to encourage us through this process.

The final day was supposed to be spent by ourselves allowing God to deal with each of us individually. No contact with each other, just each of us individually, with the Lord. The day after the final day, we could speak to each other individually or in groups, if so desired. However, if after the 21-day period any of us were still in the same emotional space with regards to our relationships (not having made much progress), we were to continue to distance ourselves from dating anyone until we were truly clear about how God would have us to move forward. Not only would these steps help with our healing, but it would also help us not to be found in, or place someone else in a rebound situation!

We became stronger in our relationship with Jesus Christ, and more intentional with our prayers. We once again realized that He needed to be at the center of every relationship, even more so in a significant other relationship. He is our source and our guide, and we have to seek him 1st.

Regardless of who contributed to the final copy of this book, we all learned something from this process and there is no doubt in our minds that 21 days was not just the beginning of us changing our lives but prayerfully all who would read this book. I thanked God for giving me (Lisa) this idea and that after writing this book we plan to participate in conferences, workshops and seminars and speak about our experiences. Ultimately, the authors hope to help people solve their problems proactively and alleviate several of the challenges that have been known to cause conflict in relationships.

Should you decide to tackle this challenge with a group of your friends, I suggest you keep it small, no more than 4 people total. The 30 minutes that you set to meet daily will pass by pretty quickly. This is a closed group, with the same individuals committed to meeting and actively participating every day. This type of group is not one where someone can choose not to engage. Each activity is required by all who are a part of the group. After identifying the friends, you want to participate, make your calls to your friends, and explain the process. Each person must agree to start the process the next day. Once all have agreed to engage in the process, start immediately! This is important because delaying the start is potentially delaying one's healing process. The more time your friends must ponder the decision, they may find ways to back out of the challenge. As you prepare, remind yourself that "You attract what's within". This is what God shared with me (Lisa) at 2:16am, the day before we had our first video call. This spoke volumes to all of us. What was within us that caused so much pain that we continued to attract more of it? We were soon to find out!

Close to the beginning of the process one of the participants asked, "Why do we keep fighting what we already know?" I (Lisa) responded, "I think when that happens it is usually because we have not hit rock bottom (which is different for everyone) or we do not really want to change yet. In our minds we may want to change but our hearts say otherwise. When the hurt, pain, grief, guilt, shame or whatever feeling we experience outweighs our desire to change, then we actually choose to change, and change does occur. Change is just as much emotional and mental as it is physical, but it is all a matter of the heart. We have to want different not just in our minds, but also in our hearts for both to work. Purging is never easy, and change can be difficult at times, but through this 21 Day No Contact Challenge we are beginning to do the work. Trust the Process."

Trusting the process is exactly what we did, with daily prayer, journaling and encouraging phone calls, texts, and other activities, we all wanted to become more intentional and aware of the types of relationships we enter in the future.

Through our daily journaling we noticed that all of us had "daddy" issues. Lisa's mom and dad separated when she was in the 4th grade and her dad moved between Maryland, DC, and Florida where her grandmother (his mother) lived. Her dad died 1 week before her senior year in high school.

Tracy's father passed away suddenly after suffering a traumatic brain injury, almost 9 years ago. He struggled with substance use disorder throughout her formative years, until she was 14 years of age. He was clean and sober 26 years at the time of his death. Though they had a close relationship, there was so much they didn't have an opportunity to experience.

It's said that a father is a female child's first way to learn how a man should treat them. The father's relationship with his daughter is her first example of a relationship with a male. When a father treats his daughter well, she will expect to be treated well by the man she is dating. Conversely, if her father is inconsistent, in and out of her life, that daughter may not have any real understanding or knowledge of how a man is supposed to treat her.

By day five, God had given me (Lisa) the idea to write about this process and share it with others, so they could also be more intentional about dating with hopes that it could prayerfully lead to healthier relationships and ultimately a sound marriage as healed individuals. The next day I shared the idea with the ladies. I was glad to hear at least three of us were immediately interested in writing about this process but more importantly, I was glad that a real bond was established between each of us.

In addition to the type of relationships we had with our fathers, we also realized we had more common ground. This is often what we used to encourage each other through the process. During our daily discussion we learned that we constantly shared about our faults with ourselves and how we made the wrong decisions, choices repeatedly. We realized that we had to forgive ourselves and replace those thoughts with new, positive things to say about ourselves instead of focusing on our failures. We repented to God for our sins, our mistakes, our actions, our thoughts, and our words and now we are replacing the negative behavior with positive behavior.

By the end of the process everyone agreed to contribute to this book, but one was not available to meet the initial deadline due to scheduling conflicts and withdrew from the process. Another had some personal challenges that prohibited her from continuing to participate. Both ladies were encouraged to write their own books when they made the time to do so. That left me (Lisa) and Tracy as the final authors of the book.

First, we wanted to collectively share some of our prior relationship experiences to give insight on how we ended up where we were. We recognized through this process that patterns were formed, and it helped us to not only acknowledge them but begin to break them and form new patterns and boundaries in our relationships. The actual names of the men in this book have been changed to nicknames (Tracy's suggestion), however, these are our true recollections. We ask that you read our stories and learn from our experiences. Our prayer is that you will begin your own 21 Days No Contact Challenge and be forever changed!

Dear Lord,

We pray for strength on this journey. Help us to depend on you. Give us all clarity of mind. Please heal us in our brokenness. Fill up the empty spaces in our hearts. Help us to grow to be the women you intended for us to be; when you formed us in our mother's wombs. Guide us to genuine love, fill us up so we feel loved. Thank you, Lord, for the ladies placed around me, you know each of us by name. Remind us that we are loved by you, we are enough, we are chosen! In Jesus' name. Amen.

Tracy M. Worley

CHAPTER 2

Trooper

I (Lisa) was introduced to my first "real" boyfriend, **Trooper** in 10th grade by one of my friends who went to Deal Junior High School with me. Both attended the same high school. Sometimes I would meet them at the Union Station subway station on my way home from Coolidge Senior High School since their school was close to where I caught my metro bus. We spoke on the phone daily, but I had an 11pm phone curfew because if I stayed up too late, I would not wake up on time for school, even with an alarm clock! With that being said, one of us would call each other after we got home from school. We would speak for a little and would get off the phone. He would call me back around 10:45pm a few minutes before my curfew to say good night. This happened almost every day, even on the afternoons we spent together. One day I asked him about that pattern. During that conversation he told me he was cheating on me. I guess the positive in that situation is that he did tell me himself instead of me having to find out on my own. I took the good with the bad and ended the relationship shortly thereafter, but we did continue to remain in contact well into my 20's.

I went to visit him in Tuskegee, Alabama on my way to my family reunion in Columbus, Georgia when I found out it was only 30 minutes away. I only visited for a couple of hours, and we did not speak much after that until we reconnected on social media years later. He was the first boyfriend who cheated on me but unfortunately, he was not the last.

Artistically Sculpted

I tried to do things differently after **Trooper** and did not date anyone for a while. I was taking a SAT class after school, and I saw this tall man with a chocolate complexion and a beautiful smile. **Artistically Sculpted** was fine! We flirted during almost every class and then one day, it happened, he gave me his phone number! I usually was eager to contact a guy after he gave me his number and I am not quite sure why I did not give him mine, but I wish I did. Nevertheless, I did not want to seem like I was "pressed" to talk to him, so I took the number and waited seven whole days before I called him! Yep, I waited until it was time for us to return to the SAT class the following week before we spoke, so he thought I was not interested. I messed that one up! Now **Artistically Sculpted** is a well-known artist, sculptor, and tattoo artist with commissioned works in DC and beyond! He is doing big things and I am super proud of him. I do not think I ever told him this but a part of me has always felt like I made the biggest mistake not contacting him shortly after he gave me his phone number. I felt this way especially because it was not because I was not interested in him, but because I was interested, and I just wanted to do something different and not rush into anything. Well, clearly seven days was seven days too long! I guess that is the reason why now I usually do not take a guy's number. Instead, I give them mine. If they call, they call, and if they don't call, they don't, that way the pressure is off of me and I am not disappointed if I never receive the call.

During the summer before my senior year in high school I began dating a friend of mine who sang in the choir with me since 10th grade. He also played on the football team. **Athletic Singer** sang a duet at my daddy's funeral with me. This was special to me because he never had the opportunity to meet my dad. **Athletic Singer** made sure I was well taken care of and looked out for me. **Athletic Singer** and I continued to date during my freshman year at Virginia Union University (VUU). For the most part, I enjoyed life at the university, however, I missed **Athletic Singer** and being able to spend quality time with him like we did when I was in DC. We would write and try to see each other as often as we could. Sometimes **Athletic Singer** would visit me when he was not scheduled to work on the weekends. He was an extremely hard worker and (still is), but he always made time for me when I came home to visit. Since quality time is my love language, that was important to me. Let's be honest, I knew nothing about love languages at that age, but I was quite aware that spending quality time with those I loved was extremely important to me. I was always a priority in **Athletic Singer**'s life, and we tried our best to make our long-distance relationship work. I loved him tremendously and thought for a moment, he would be my forever love. Funny thing is, he wanted to marry me. I was not ready for marriage at that time, but I was also not interested in dating anyone else. Besides, he nor I had any idea of the obstacles we would have to face in the future.

On Labor Day weekend about a month after arriving at VUU the curfew was extended. I was supposed to attend a concert with friends on Sunday night but since I was a music major, my choir director told me that I had to sing in the concert the university choir was asked to participate in that same evening. I sold my ticket to the concert and when I arrived back to Richmond, I found out that the concert the choir was supposed to sing in was canceled. It was a holiday weekend, and I was bored so when **Basketball Player** asked me to hang out with him, I was happy to get out of the dorm. Besides, I did not think it would be a problem because **Athletic Singer** and I often hung out with people of the opposite sex. Furthermore, he was the only man I was romantically interested in at that time. I did not think there would be a problem, nor did I expect anything to happen, but I still decided to tell some of my friends where I was going. You see, in our college freshman class, they always said to let someone know where you were going for safety purposes. This time it did not keep me safe!

Basketball Player came to my dormitory to walk me back to the basketball house where he lived. We talked about almost everything, but I wanted him to clearly know that I was just hanging out with him, and whenever I shared any information, my discussion was mainly about **Athletic Singer.** Clearly, **Basketball Player** did not care. More dialogue was exchanged and as we were sitting on the side of the bed (that was the only furniture in the room) he began giving me a host of compliments and tried to caress me. I pulled away. *Trigger warning- graphic, details ahead.* The next thing I know, he was on top of me! He was kissing me, but I moved my head and did not kiss him back instead I said, "Please stop- no!" Various thoughts were going through my head. "How did all of this begin?" "Weren't we just talking about my boyfriend and how much I loved *him*?" He used his size and strength to pin me down with one hand and used his other hand to move my panties to the side while licking my ears and neck. I tried to get up, but I could not! He disregarded any of my pleas for him to stop and continued doing what he wanted to do to me. Even though my legs were strong I couldn't move them, it was as if I were paralyzed, limp.

Next thing I know he has placed several fingers inside of me and proceeded to insert his penis, without a condom, inside of me! This was no joke; he was raping me! I was ashamed, discouraged, and I guess in shock, because I could not scream or say anything initially when he started. I felt like a child that hadn't even learned to speak yet. Somehow, I was able to say an entire sentence, "If you don't stop I am going to scream," but I was unable to scream. At any rate, nothing else I tried to say would come out of my mouth. I guess he could see the disgust on my face because after a short while he stopped. I tried to compose myself, not knowing whether to laugh or cry (those are my usual defense or coping mechanisms in uncomfortable situations) and after I got myself together, he walked me back to my dorm as if nothing had occurred at all. Years later when I was seeing a counselor and I mentioned the rape, she told me, "You lost your voice". That was the first time that I felt like someone really was empathetic and understood what I might have felt in that moment.

As **Basketball Player** walked me back to my dorm, I was quiet. Maybe I was in shock, but I had pretty much decided that there was no way I could press charges, not against him, the well-known basketball player. In addition to that, I did not think anyone would believe me if they found out that I stated a complete sentence but was not able to scream. How could I explain that? I didn't want to deal with the press or any court case. I literally had only been in college for less than 1 month at that point. I was attending my university to get an education; I was not there to get raped!

When I returned to my dorm, my friends asked how my evening was. I covered my pain by laughing and telling them I had fun and that he kisses well. Yes, I did lie about having fun and what I thought about his kisses so that they would not ask any more questions about the evening. Inside I was torn about reporting it and I wanted to take a shower. I felt so ashamed and stupid! Going to that university was supposed to be the beginning of the rest of my life (so to speak) and there was absolutely nothing that was going to change that. While I was in the shower, tears began rolling down my cheeks. I tried to wash the pain I felt down the drain and remembered each terrifying action. The emotional scars that took place because of the rape were so painful. As I cried myself to sleep, I became aware just how much that rape could have affected the rest of my life.

A day or so after the rape, something strange happened. I received a phone call from one of my cousins. I was upset and tried to hide the fact that I was crying while I was sitting on the floor talking on the payphone. I did not want anyone in their rooms to hear me so I was speaking as softly as I could. I guess he could tell that something was wrong and asked me if I was okay. I began telling him what happened to me, and he was furious that someone would hurt me like that. I asked my cousin not to tell my family about the incident. About two weeks after my cousin called me, he mailed me this letter:

September 17, xxxx

"Lisa, I really feel compelled to write to you now during this time of need, since I haven't been to sleep for two days worrying about you. Every time I think about what happened to you, I just get more and more angry. Partly because I am in a situation where I can't help you 'cause I can't reach you ... I mean, I know I've done some terrible things in my life, but that's truly beyond my limits! I don't understand it!!

But not to make matters any worse than they already are. I truly admire your strength and courage. It takes a strong person with a lot of will power to be able to bounce back as you are doing, especially in the same environment. If you ever feel yourself in a life-threatening position in someone else's hand, then Please! Please! Please! Bring you red-ass home!! Okay? I say this only because I love you and I don't want anything to happen to you. I wish I were there."

This letter was quite confusing to me because he was one of the cousins (yes there was more than one) who molested and sexually abused me when I was a child. Then at the same time, he was the most helpful to me that night even though he violated me when I was a child. It was the weirdest thing. I found myself repressing and suppressing so many aspects of my past. For years I had mixed emotions of love and hatred towards my relatives for their actions. I loved them because they were my family but hated them for what they did to me. I thought I was supposed to be able to trust my family, but I could not. When my cousin was arrested later in life for an unrelated incident, I would go and visit him in jail. It was like I separated what he did to me from supporting family as I would any other person. Crazy, right?

Last year I was looking at a photo on the wall of me and my family celebrating his high school graduation. I had the biggest epiphany on that day. Why was I made to go to that celebration? Young or not, I should have been asked whether or not I wanted to be there, but I do not remember if that was the case. I was a child, and I did what the adults in my family told me to do, without question. It made me think, in retrospect, that was the first time I kept associating with someone who took advantage of me. Relative or not, his actions caused me pain. I confronted my cousin while speaking to him when I was in my 20's and his response? He told me that, "He did not burst my cherry"! I cried. How could my cousin be so callous? I have no idea. I have no recollection of me mentioning anything to my other cousin or his mother about him molesting me until well into my 40's. At least he did apologize. Nevertheless, I decided that I no longer wanted to be associated with him on a social level other than informing him about the funeral arrangements for my mom when she died. He was her cousin too and I was not going to allow what he did to me as a teenager to hinder him from attending her celebration of life. That was a bit difficult for me, but I was able to do it. This also meant no longer attending some family dinners or functions on holidays, which, truth be told, made holidays quite lonely. I have come to realize that although I talked about the incidents and forgave them for what they did, I was not healed yet. I was not even aware that what I had experienced was a form of trauma!

This is why I was caught by surprise by his comment in the letter. Did he not remember what he did to me when he was in junior high school? Didn't he know what he did to me was wrong as well? How could he think that what he did was any different than what **Basketball Player** did to me? I did not understand completely where he was coming from, but I do know that there were several nights that I found myself crying because of the emotional pain I was feeling. Have you ever had a pain so deep that you did not know what to do with it? I wish I could have seen the wound so I could put ointment on it so it could heal faster or make the pain go away completely, but there was no visible scar, just emotional scars, and pain. Never in a million years did I think he or anyone else would do that to me. No one ever thinks this will happen to them. What is worse, is the feelings that I held inside eventually turned into bitterness and strife against **Basketball Player** and anger at times towards God for allowing this to happen. Being sexually abused and molested by multiple family members was enough, now this? I know that I was supposed to forgive **Basketball Player,** but I was hurting and I felt that my feelings and actions were vindicated not realizing that I was only hurting myself. In essence, I am a strong proponent of forgiveness, but to be honest, making the choice to forgive **Basketball Player** for what he did to me was a much harder task. I had to work on the process of forgiving him for what he did to me, but eventually, I did forgive him.

All my struggles related to the rape were not over. I had yet another obstacle to overcome- telling my boyfriend **Athletic Singer** about what happened. I was full of anxiety and apprehensive to tell the one I loved, about what happened to me. Almost a month passed before I saw him in person. I did not want to tell him about the rape over the telephone or in a letter. Thus, whenever we spoke, I would have to act like everything was ok. That was hard, but somehow, I did it. In retrospect, I am not sure that was a good idea, since initially

24

he blamed me for what occurred. I did not appreciate him blaming me, but while researching more about rape I read that often loved-ones, mates, or spouses of those who are raped blame the victims as a way to displace their own anger. Reading this information somewhat helped me deal with his reaction, but it presented another difficulty in our relationship that probably hurt us more than any amount of distance ever could. Each time he would come to my college to visit, he would want to know who the person was who raped me. I would not tell him because I did not want him to do something that he would later regret. Eventually we were able to move past that situation but I ended the relationship the summer after my freshman year of college, but it was not easy for me to move on because of our love for each other. We were in a relationship for 1 year and 11 months, sadly my longest committed relationship to date. It was not easy for me to move on because of our love for each other. In retrospect, there were some things that I needed to work out on my own. We continued to remain cool and years later as adults his brother asked me to sing at their father's funeral and I was glad I was able to be there for them, just like **Athletic Singer** had been there for me and my family years prior when my father and grandmother died. We may not have made it as a "forever" couple, but we shared a lot of fun times together with each other and our families. I am extremely happy that now **Athletic Singer** is truly, in his own words, living his best life!

Spiritual Mister went to the same university as me. He was a few years older, and we did not have any classes together, but our conversation was dope and we definitely had chemistry. At any rate, I am not sure if he is really a preacher or a deacon in the church, but he was always preaching to me! What began as friends ended up in a sexual relationship. I found out he was not interested in a committed relationship with me although I wanted to be in one with him. What he was interested in was sex. Both of us were saved and knew that should not be the case. In fact, you would find both of us at the altar on Sunday crying out to God about what we did. We would talk about it too. I was his "secret" and although I did not like it, I stayed in my place and played my role. He never actually called me his secret, but I recall the time he asked me to leave out of the back door so that no one could see that I stayed there overnight. I ran into a fellow classmate on the way out of the house. I do not think he ever said anything but by the mere fact that someone saw me, I was no longer a secret. I am not sure why he did not want anyone to know that we were dating each other since there was no commitment. Maybe it was because he was a Christian and was ashamed of his actions. Who knows? Later on, he mentioned a conversation he had with someone about not engaging in sex with a friend because it can ruin the friendship. The level of our relationship (committed or not) was so much more than that. One day he asked me to go out with him and one of his friends. I told him that I did not have any extra money at the moment, and he said he would pay for me, and I could pay him back later. Basically, he was using me as his trophy. He wanted to show off in front of his friend like he and I were a couple but that was not the case, but I did not say anything. Sadly, I got used to not saying anything when I was asked to keep or remain a secret. That is something that seemed to happen quite often in my life. At any rate, one day I looked down the street and I saw that his brand-new car had been damaged as if it had been in an accident. I was concerned and when I tried to call him, he did not answer. At that time, I thought about if something happened to him no one would even think to notify me because no one other than his roommates knew that we were seeing each other. He later told me that someone had hit his vehicle and he was not injured. Shortly after that we stopped seeing each other but we remained friends, if that is what you want to call it. We both moved from the neighborhood we lived in, and he would call and visit me after work sometimes. He did not want to be in a relationship with me and started dating another woman, but still wanted to have sex with me. I was no longer interested, and he respected my decision or so I thought. Years later I drove one of my friends to see his girlfriend in the same city **Spiritual Mister** had moved to and visited him. Unfortunately, I did not stop to get some food before going to his house. While I was waiting for my friend to call me and let me know he was ready to return home, I became hungry. However, **Spiritual Mister's** home faced the woods, and it was late so I was a little afraid to leave the house. The city he lived in was known for its racism towards Black people. He would not go with me to get anything to eat and said there were some peaches in the freezer that I could thaw out. At that point I was willing to eat almost anything! The peaches took a while to thaw out and when they were ready, he brought them into the room I was in and began feeding them to me. He was still in a relationship so why was he doing that? Was it because he was a man? Not only did he try to feed me the peaches, but he also tried to force me to have sex! He knew what happened to me in my past and he was trying to do the same thing. I was hurt by his actions. I am more than just sex! To this day, I do not remember him ever apologizing for his actions. He eventually married his girlfriend and moved back to the city where I met him. I have not seen him much over the years but did see him at a funeral not too long ago. We spoke but in the back of my mind, I was triggered and reminded about our past. He did not have many positive things to say about me or was very rarely supportive of me. I never felt like I was good enough for him and seeing that he too married someone else, maybe I was right. It was like he never really wanted me to win and yet now he gives me compliments and kudos on social media. Go figure...

HOW DO YOU KNOW? written by Lisa Louise Gilliam

How do you know if someone really cares?

How do you know if they'll always be there?

These are questions I asked myself a lot

but before I receive an answer, I must tell you my plot.

Have you ever seen a face that could make you smile?

Have you ever seen a face that could make you laugh?

Well, a young man I met in college, does not matter his name
seemed to do this to me and warm my insides just the same.

It was sad however, the path that he would take

not choosing me as his girlfriend, but selling drugs as his stake.

And although not doing so overtly,

He said things that would hurt me.

Jokes such as I could not have his baby, I was too

T

A

L

L

Did this mean he did not care about me at all?

When you care about someone, you accept them for them,

Just as I accepted him for him

and the things he did, even when I didn't agree.

There was never a fault too big or too small.

I cared so much about him, my feelings couldn't express

How I wished we could be together in sweet gentleness.

How do I know if he really cares?

How do I know if he'll always be there?

Or

Does it matter to him now,

that I'm leaving anyhow?

Is this the end of a beautiful thing

Or will it bring me a wedding ring?

No matter how much I wish we could be together

Through rain, sunshine or windy weather

I don't want his child or anyone else's

I don't think it was stupid for me to think so mildly

About wanting him to be with only me

And share the joy that can be-

I mean exist between a friend and a lover-

I've finally come to my senses and it's now time for me to leave you alone, my brother.

Football Hustler

My junior year in college I dated a football player by day and hustler by night who was a few years younger than me. He was tall and there was an immediate attraction on both parts. We were in an art class together and he started flirting with me. I should have known he was going to be trouble when he asked me to take him to his off-campus apartment when by all accounts he actually stayed on campus. On the way back to drop him off I got a ticket. I cannot remember if it was for speeding or running a red light. I did end up having to go to court before I could pay the ticket. It was such an inconvenience!

He was charming and funny. After a while I began to really like him a lot. How do I know? I can cook but do not enjoy cooking and I would cook him home cooked meals, like fried chicken with a vegetable and a starch at 10pm and then take it to his dorm because he did not have a car then. One day he got a ride to my apartment and as soon as he entered, he placed a gun on my table. That rattled me a bit. I suspected that he might've been hustling but that night he basically confirmed it without confirming it. Prior to that I was not completely sure because he usually kept that side from me. Nonetheless, we dated off and on during my junior and senior year and after I graduated, I was considering applying to a college in Richmond to get my master's degree if he had wanted me to do so just to remain in the same town with him. The long and short of this story is that is not what he wanted.

After I went home to DC, he mentioned to me that he slept with one of my former roommates. That was a shocker and quite hurtful! I was wondering why she was being so mean to me out of the blue. Maybe it was because of guilt. I do not remember if I ever asked her if that really happened between them or not, but I did know that she never spoke to me again. You would have thought I did something to her instead of the other way around. This guy was one of many that I dated that did not want a commitment with me but went on to marry someone else. We still have a connection on social media, and we do keep in contact from time to time. I usually see him when I go to my college homecoming.

Southern Entrepreneur once told me after we stopped dating that I was more attractive than the new lady he was dating. When we stopped dating, we continued to stay in touch, but he failed to tell me when he made the decision to marry her! I was actually dating **Slow Cooker** and was not thinking about him in a romantic way any longer, nor had I been for months. That is why I did not understand why he would not tell me that he had decided to settle down especially since we were only friends. What hurt even more is I found out that he now has children. That hurt because when we were dating, he told me he did not want any children, but I always did. I was flabbergasted! Before I found out **Southern Entrepreneur** was married, I called to check on him since we had not spoken in a while. He waited to return my call and did so late one night. Now I do not think I would have been happy if I had married him, but why was he not real with me instead of sneaking to return my call after his wife was asleep? There was no reason to sneak a return call. Maybe he should have been honest with his now wife about how he felt about me before he married her but then again, that might have ended his marriage plans.

About Slow Cooker written by Lisa Louise Gilliam

He is a master in the kitchen, but did I mention everything he does is nice?

His touch is sensual, and his kisses are like sugar and spice

With each passing day, my heart grows fonder, and my expectations are being fulfilled

The more we communicate and spend time together our true feelings are being revealed

Now there are sweet memories and passionate responses, can all of this be true?

Yes, seeing YOU is always like a breath of fresh air...Wow, can YOU feel that breeze too?

I often wrote poems or songs to express my feelings. Sometimes I shared them with the public and sometimes I wrote them to get my own thoughts out of my head. This was one of the poems I wrote about **Slow Cooker** when we were dating. I was on the planning committee for my 20-year high school class reunion and **Slow Cooker**, one of the guys that I never even spoke to while we were in high school, told me I caught his eye! He was a handsome guy and what was only supposed to be one conversation to tell him what he needed to do in order to pay for the reunion turned into several lengthy laughter filled conversations. At the reunion he walked up to greet me and touched the small of my back. Literally it was electric. Later we both asked each other if we felt the same thing, we did! I had never felt anything like that from a simple touch, from anyone! We definitely had chemistry!

After the reunion we remained in touch and **Slow Cooker** asked if he could take me out as a "thank you" date for helping him with the reunion. It turned out to be a fabulous dinner date at Copper Canyon. He shared so much about himself with me that night, things I definitely did not expect to learn on a first date, but I appreciated his honesty. It was a great date and he made me giddy! We both enjoyed laughing, watching movies, and listening to music. I remember how when we began dating, he used to play "Caught My Eye" by Mint Condition all the time, a reminder of how I caught his eye. That became our song.

We talked about our individual future plans, dreams, goals and I had the chance to meet and spend time with some of his family and he met some of mine as well. He was romantic and boy could that guy cook! I fell hard for **Slow Cooker**. I had been cheated on previously, so it was important to me that we had an agreement. If he ever decided to date or get in a relationship with someone else, he would tell me first. I did not want to be surprised if things changed. I am not exactly sure when things changed, when he stopped being as forthcoming with information about himself as he had been since our 1st date, but things changed.

We did not speak for a week or so, which was unlike us. He ghosted me! Then when we did have a conversation, I asked him directly what was going on and if we were still dating and he said we were, but something did not feel right. The person I thought I knew; was not the person I knew at all. What is crazy is there were not too many people that knew that we dated or that things were as serious as they were between us. He never asked me to keep us a secret. In fact, he posted photos of us together on social media first. He mentioned me to his best friends long before I ever told anyone about us dating. We were always together so later when his words changed from, I love you to I have love for you, I was crushed! It had been 15 years since I "fell" for a guy like that! He knew that and for him to lie and change up on me like that was heartbreaking. What was even worse, is I found out he was dating someone else because one of the individuals was a mutual friend who called to tell me that she thinks she was dating someone I was dating. When I questioned him about this, I found out that it was the truth and there were other females he was dating as well. Things did not end until I gathered enough strength to stop desiring something I would not get from the man who once said he loved me.

There was so much more that happened after all I endured with **Slow Cooker** but since I never shared it then, I will spare you all the details and not share it now. It is crazy to think that although my relationship with **Slow Cooker** was not a secret relationship like some had been in my past, there was a time that I was a secret because none of the females involved with him knew who he was dating and when until after it happened. In retrospect, instead of loving out loud and just keeping their secrets, in several of my relationships I became their secret. This is not something I am proud of, nor is it something I was even aware of when it was happening. I am aware of it now and it shall not be repeated again! Needless to say, **Slow Cooker** broke my heart! I know people change their minds about who they want to date all the time, but it is always best to communicate that information instead of just leaving things in the air. I needed to express my feelings and I wrote the lyrics below initially calling the song, "I Give Up On Love". I changed my mind and decided that I was not going to let how he treated me or what he did to me cause me not to love again and changed the title to "I Give Up On Us". I haven't recorded the song yet, but I may do so if I ever record my R&B CD. I did enter the song in a music contest where I was selected as a finalist. If you would like to hear it, check it out on my Youtube.com/OneSingingLady page.

I Give Up On Us written by Lisa Louise Gilliam

Chorus

I give up on us, don't know what else to say

I give up on us, don't come around me another day

I knew you had a past, but I didn't think you'd treat me that way

So, I give up on us

The pain I feel is real, the hurt I cannot describe

And all I do is cry both day and night oh

Just can't believe you treated me that way, won't even take my phone calls

Wish you had the nerve to face me, but you won't do that at all so,

I give up on us, don't know what else to say

I give up on us, don't talk to me another day

I knew you had a past, but I didn't think you'd treat me that way

So, I give up on us

So many memories, seem to flood my mind

And where we've ended up is strange because to me you were so kind

Feels like an arrow was shot and pierced through my heart

And though I love you, your actions are tearing us apart so

I give up on us, don't know what else to say

I give up on us, don't come around or talk to me another day

I knew you had a past, but I didn't think you'd treat me that way

So, I give up on us

Bridge

In the pit of my soul, I feel bitter and cold

Don't know how you could do this to me

Said you loved me, but now I disagree

Guess it was something you said, to get what you wanted

So, I give up on us, although I thought you truly loved me

It is such as shame that now our plans have changed

This is the end

We are over we are through

I must move on now; I know what I have to do

Look out for me and that's what matters

We are done, I give up on us

After all of that, **Slow Cooker** began dating one of the females exclusively and she ended up becoming his wife. I was not even mad about his decision to get married. It was all the other things that happened that left me broken-hearted. Truth is, I have always wished nothing but the best for **Slow Cooker** nor do I hold any ill feelings towards him. He may have made some poor choices when we dated, but that was years ago, and I have accepted his apology. I also decided to see a counselor so I could process all that had taken place. Here I was again dating a guy that decided to marry someone else. Moreover, it started to feel like I was the woman who prepared men to marry the next woman after dating me. By the time it happened when I was dating **Slow Cooker** I was getting tired of it! Arrgggg…. Then again, that meant that I was not the one for them, or that they were not willing to be honest with themselves about why they married the individual that they married. You would be surprised what I would find out during counseling sessions with my clients. I never knew so many people would marry for money (men and women), or just because they were lonely regardless of if the person was the "right" one or not.

Dead Liar

This tall, attractive guy slipped into my inbox and after a few conversations he asked for a date. We made plans and he stood me up! He told the first lie to me after that. I honestly think he was dating someone else but since we were not together, I let it slide. He was always out with someone and posting pics. Eventually, we met up for drinks. He had a hangover, so when I say drinks, I actually mean iced tea. I honestly think he did not have the money to pay for whatever I wanted to order. The next year and a half I went through so many things with him. There were constant lies, like all the time. I later found out that he did not just lie to me but lied to other women too. He lied about where he lived, where he worked, his relationships and so much more. Me being the forgiving person that I am forgave him for what he said and what he did. One time I bought him lunch from a burger spot I liked. He and I had a discussion and decided we were going to date exclusively to find out if we wanted to be in a committed relationship. The next day I called to say hi. No answer. In fact, he did not answer the entire week! Then at the end of the week he invited me over to talk in person. I had no idea what he wanted to discuss. Although I had reservations, I went to go see him. He tells me that he and his ex-girlfriend decided to reconnect. I had no idea he was even dating anyone else. Months later I received a text that said although they decided to date, he still wanted to see me too. I still liked him. We had chemistry; you do the math. That was Deja vu. He and that girl broke up and then he was with someone else. I was not a priority, even when it was discussed that I would be...wrong decision again. He told another mutual friend he did not plan on coming to any of my events. There were so many other things that this guy did to me but eventually, I realized my worth and did not want to be 1 of the many women that he was seeing. This guy is now dead, literally. All the lies he told to me and so many others who were not aware of the lies he shared are now buried along with him.

Graphic Visionary and I met when we were on the usher board at Turner Memorial AME, my childhood church. I affectionately called him my "Usherman" for that reason. Our families knew each other, and I found out right before we started dating that he attended the same high school as I did but graduated years before me. Funny enough I also found out that he and **Dead Liar** graduated from that school in the same year! It was a small world. We got re-connected on social media and I invited him to come to hear me sing one evening. He did, and the rest was history! He was attentive and kind. In my opinion, he shined! The lyrics to" Shining Star", a song I wrote prior to us dating, reminds me of how I often felt when **Graphic Visionary** and I were dating. I haven't officially recorded the song yet, but if I do decide to record again in the studio this is one of the songs I want to add to my R&B CD.

<u>Shining Star</u> written by Lisa Louise Gilliam

(Spoken) When I'm with you, the world's a much brighter place :-) you shine

Chorus-You're my shining star shining bright so all the world can see through darkness

You light up my life, you 're my destiny please don't take your light away from me

I am moved to no end about the kindness you share, though rare, it is so precious

Like a diamond in the rough you pulled me out of a dry place and gave me life again (gave me life again)

It's like coming up for air after being under water that's how it feels to me

You're my knight in shining armor, keeping me safe, that's what you do for me

and with each passing moment I think of you more and more

So grateful you're in my life, I've got a lot to be thankful for…

Chorus

I am overjoyed when I hear your voice, it's so soothing, the way you speak to me

Like fireworks ignited when our lips touch so much passion I can't even explain (I can't even explain)

It's like we're on a tropical island without ever leaving town
that's how it feels to me

You're an inspiration, pure delight is what you bring to me

and with each passing moment I think of you more and more

So grateful you're in my life, I've got a lot to be thankful for…

Chorus

It did not take long for me to love **Graphic Visionary**. When I love, I love hard and loving **Graphic Visionary** was no different but there were also times of disconnect. He would say I was his muse, but I felt like I was a bystander sometimes. He was focused on his work and since we were in a relationship, I longed for him to focus a bit more on us.

<u>Graphic Visionary Poem</u> written by Lisa Louise Gilliam

If I am your muse let me also be your paper

write what's on your mind and every moment I'll savor

Just glimpses of your thoughts are worth more than a penny

I wish our conversations were in depth although we've had many

I laid a lot on you tonight and understand you need your time

But real talk, I wish-

I could squeeze some info from you like I would a lime

I am out of rhyming words...have nothing else to say

Except I hope things soon get better for both of us, baby.

I knew **Graphic Visionary** loved me, but I did not feel like I was a priority in his life more often than not. I shared this with him, but we still drifted apart. Quality time is my love language and that is not what we were spending. In addition, he was primarily a quiet person and I often felt like I had to "pull" information out of him, even the simplest information that would normally be shared by individuals in a relationship. **Graphic Visionary** and I officially dated for about 8 months but continued to date off and on for a while after we broke up. It literally took me about 4 years to completely move forward and want to be in a committed relationship with another guy. Honestly, I really did not want our relationship to end, and I still loved him even after we broke up. I also think that since we continued to date for so long, even after the relationship ended, in the back of my mind I had hoped that we might get back together again. That did not happen. Although we did not work out as a couple, I can say that out of all of my ex-boyfriends, he was the only one that was still in my corner, actively wished me well, celebrated my wins or if necessary, listened when I was having difficulties in life. That meant the world to me.

After **Graphic Visionary** and I broke up, my dating life remained the same; empty! There always seemed to be someone interested in me but there was no action following their supposed interest. Until I became reconnected with my friend, **M and M**.

Instead of becoming a soft landing, only someone to talk to whenever **M and M** had a rough moment, I became his escape from his everyday life. There is a difference regarding being a soft landing, a friendly and supportive ear and becoming an escape, a place where he not only landed but dwelled for a while, unhindered or unbothered. **M and M** and I knew each other for a while and although there was always an attraction on both of our parts, I knew I was not his first choice and since I was only an option that kept me away from giving in to any of the advances, he made towards me. How did I know that I wasn't his first choice? He was married! Although I never married, I had been cheated on before and I didn't want anyone else to experience that kind of pain. Then, one day I found myself vulnerable and in a lot of pain of my own. I was being verbally and at times physically abused by a relative. I was accused of doing things that I did not do, and it was hurtful. No matter how many times I denied the accusations, the person did not believe me. There was so much going on in my life and I didn't feel supported by family or friends most of the time.

M and M gave me the support and attention I desired that I didn't receive from others. Our conversations turned into lunch dates on occasion. Those lunch dates led to him asking me to be sexually intimate with him. I was able to say no for quite some time, but our conversations and the familiarity ultimately led me to become his mistress. That outcome, however, was unexpected, at least for me. I never thought I would give in to his requests, but I did and I was falling in love with him. If you don't completely put the fire out when it's burning, it might reignite when you least expect it. Think about it, if there were a fire and it wasn't completely burned out, those embers could reignite again. It was clear to me that our flames from when we first met (remember I mentioned that we knew each other for a while) never completely burned out. Besides, it was easy to continue to spend time with him because we were supporting each other through what we were individually enduring in our own lives. I was experiencing financial hardship and he gave me money to help with extra expenses. He also listened to me when I needed to vent. When I was angry or hurt, he comforted me. He was there for me during a period of isolation when I felt so alone. My parents and grandparents were deceased by that time. I have 1 younger sibling who would call and check on me, but he had his own family responsibilities to attend to and I needed additional support.

It was **M and M** who encouraged me to get out of the house and go for a walk with him when I felt anxious or depressed. I was in a lot of emotional pain and there was so much chaos going on, but he was a constant in my life at that time. Then, I had to come to the reality that he was not a constant either. He could only be there for me when he was not with her. Besides, sin is sin and fornication (sex outside the confines of marriage) is sin according to what the Bible says. I felt all kinds of guilt and shame during the time that we were involved. The truth was **M and M** was all of what I wanted and none of what I needed.

I usually maintained friendships with my ex's, but that was not an easy task for either of us, so I began counseling again and tried to distance myself from **M and M** to heal and move forward once and for all. I didn't want to be available for a deposit from him or any other man when I wouldn't get a return on my investment. I was more valuable than that!

We genuinely had to "fight" not to call or text even if it were just to check on each other. It was a miserable feeling to want to completely be with someone who was knowingly sharing his time with someone else. I thought about not speaking about this because of the shame I felt, but it's a part of my life so I'm including these details. Let me be clear, I didn't write this book to get back at anyone. I wrote it to shed light on how trauma led me to make some horrible dating choices. It is my prayer that what I have learned thus far and continue to learn about my past choices and decisions will equip me to become better for whomever God sends to find me and ask for my hand in marriage.

Part of me decided to take this 21 Days No Contact Challenge so I could heal from all past hurts and not make those decisions or mistakes again. The other part of me wanted to encourage the reader that no matter how bad your choices have been in your life, if God allows you to see another day, you too can repent, ask Him for forgiveness and try again. Even when you have forgiven someone for what they did, that does not necessarily take away the pain immediately. It can be a process. However, sometimes the person that you must forgive first is yourself. In my case, my pain was still present, and my heart had to line up with my determination to change. If I changed my heart, truly desiring to live a life that was pleasing to God, my mind would follow suit. This didn't mean that I wouldn't make mistakes or never sin again, but it did mean that I wanted and was willing (my heart and thoughts) to change and do something about it (my actions). Thus, as wrong as our actions were, if this never happened, I may not have realized how my past played an important role in my decisions with relationships, not just with him, but with other men I dated prior to him, as well as my friendships. I made so many grave errors in judgment.

Word to the Wise always had a way with words! He was my wordsmith. He knew what to say to me and how to say it. Literally,

I would blush because of some of the things he said, none of which were ever disrespectful. Whenever we spoke, we connected on a cerebral level, and I appreciated that. We've had some great conversations via phone, and he would text me often to check on my well-being, shower me with compliments, or simply encourage me to have a wonderful day when our work schedules didn't allow us to see each other in person. I believed his words about his interest in me were sincere, but he never asked me out on an official date! That was disheartening because I also believe that if you are interested in someone, you should show them that you want to be in their presence and find time to spend with them. I am past dating just to date; I want to get married. So, unless a guy is willing to make a plan and spend quality time with me, stimulate my mind, call me daily, yes, I really mean daily, then I am not interested in seriously dating or being in a committed relationship with that person. At any rate **Word to the Wise** was a nice guy and I guess only time will tell what happens next.

As you can see, I have experienced several types of relationships, some were pleasant, and some weren't. Those experiences have led me to think about the things that have happened in my life, to include my own choices and the actions forced upon me. For instance, almost every Labor Day weekend since the rape happened, I am reminded of that incident. Sometimes it triggers me and sometimes I'm fine. Life experiences are funny that way. Now, I understand that much of my behavior was a direct correlation because of my past. That does not excuse nor justify my behavior or choices.

Nonetheless, if you know anything about trauma, being a victim of abuse, etc., you know that there are things that become learned behavior when those type of things happen to you. I found out that past trauma, sexual abuse, molestation, and rape was a part of the reason for how I allowed myself to be treated, as well as the behavior I exhibited. I have forgiven myself now. I have no doubt that although God wasn't pleased with what I did, He already knew I wouldn't be obedient to His will at that time. He knew that I would sin in that manner, and yet He loved me anyway. I'm so grateful! He still called me to be a minister of His Gospel. One day when more healing has taken place, I will continue to do just that. I realized how important resting, spending quiet time by myself and in prayer with my creator, God, was and has always been essential.

I learned that I deserve to be a priority. If I'm not, it's more than okay for me to move on. I will never be an option again. I didn't realize my worth in the past, but I certainly know it now! I will date with intention (marriage). Some refer to this as courting and not dating. I also set boundaries and have decided I only want to have relationships with individuals who want me in their lives. This is for all types of relationships-friendships, romantic relationships, and even familial relationships. This has made me a better individual and I continue to heal from the past trauma I've experienced. I look forward to seeing what God has in store for me next!

I remember trying to numb the pain and fill the voids with actions that were not pleasing to Christ. I knew this. I have taught this, and I have lived by this...until I didn't. Without a doubt I know that no matter how old I become, I need to draw on Jesus for strength and nothing can numb the pain or fill the voids in my life -not sex, not substances, not people, not things, nothing, except Jesus.Before I go, I want to leave you with this. When I was in undergraduate school at VUU, I changed my major from Vocal Music Performance to Speech and Drama. We had several productions that went on each year. I would like for you to imagine, if you will, that you are a part of a theater production. Everyone, which means the stagehands, lighting, and sound crew, as well as the actors and actresses, in a theater production has to know what's going on from the director. One slow cue from the stagehand to the actors can cause them to miss a line. If the lighting director did not bring the lights up on time, that could cause them to be in the dark or exposed on stage before they were supposed to be there. Now, if there is a puppet in the show there is also a puppet master. The puppet master does not tell the puppet what they're going to do, they do it for them. They pull their strings, make them move, dance, etc., so that they're doing what they're supposed to be doing in the theater production.

Also, imagine the promoter's job. If they didn't do their job the seats might not be filled, then there would be no one present to see the theater production. Conversely, the promoter might have promoted the theater production well so that the tickets sold out. In one case, there's no support for the show and in the other, there is support. Usually, the seats closest to the stage cost the most. You must pay a higher price for those seats. They can be expensive and sometimes they may even come with perks like a VIP (Very Important Person) benefit. Those people who sit in those front row seats had to do something different to get there. They had to count the cost and if they wanted to sit in those front row seats, pay the price.

The theater production is YOUR life! In your production do you know all the key players so that the foundation of the production goes off well? In live theater there are always mistakes or mishaps because we are human. However, is everyone on your team on the same page or are you the puppet that has been controlled by a puppet master, and only knows a portion of what is supposed to be happening in your own theater production (life)? Did you let someone sit in the front row of your life that didn't count the cost or pay a high price to sit there? If the theater production of YOUR life is based on a solid foundation, all players are informed of what direction the director, God, wants the production to go. If an individual you are dating tells you they aren't ready for a relationship now, but you know in your heart of hearts that's what you want, stop dealing with them immediately! They're telling you what they want, so unless they change their mind, don't set yourself up for a failed (life) theater production. If there's no commitment and communication, there's no way there will be a solid foundation or theater production (life).

I have never met anyone who wants to attend a horrible theater production, just as I have never met anyone who wants to have a horrible life! From this point on, please don't let your life become a horrible theater experience with you, as the star, in a position where someone else is pulling your strings. Please share your intentions and directions of the theater production with the leading characters, supporting cast, and production team so that you have a solid foundation and the support you need along the way to make your production a success. More importantly, please seek God to find out who all the key players of your production really are before you begin the theater production in the first place!!

You may be like me in your late 40's with a broken past. Then one day it hit me like a ton of bricks! I was right where I was supposed to be and so are you! God already knew everything I was going to do, good, bad, indifferent…. It was not about if God will heal, deliver, or bless, it was about the fact that He is able to do it whether He chooses to do so or not, and is still worthy of praise. I want you to know that if you've had failed relationships or experienced abuse, rape, etc., you may have been broken, but you are not destroyed! Furthermore, you are still valuable to God and those who truly love you. Think about owning a valuable, expensive, crystal vase that was an heirloom passed down to you or something else expensive that you purchased or now own. Then one day, someone drops it, and it breaks, cracks, or chips. It doesn't matter if it were done on purpose or by accident, more than likely you would want to preserve it because it was worth something to you.

Most people who truly treasure something don't say oh, well, I am just going to throw it away. Instead, we try to fix it first. Too many people are throwing away their lives because they think they are broken and beyond repair. I want you to know that although you might be broken, you are not shattered. When something is shattered it's in so many pieces that it may be beyond repair. On the contrary, broken pieces can be put back together again. Please don't take my word for it. Look up broken and shattered in the dictionary and see for yourself. Instead of throwing away your life, begin repairing what has been broken. I truly believe that God wants to fix our hurt, our pain, our heartache, etc. but we must give it all to him instead of turning to material things, substances. or improper relationships and experiences with people that don't want God's best for us. Remember, regardless of what has happened in our lives, you and I will always be valuable to God.

CHAPTER 3

In order to assess my patterns of behavior as it relates to relationships, I (Tracy) must go back to the beginning. How did all of this get started for me? Simply wanting to be loved is how I got here.

I am a hopeless romantic and have been for a very long time. I am the girl who had a subscription to Bride's magazine before I graduated from High School, because I loved weddings so much. I was in love with the idea of what love looked like to me. I was naïve when it came to love and relationships. I have seen relationships modeled before me. Both sets of grandparents, my father and stepmother, and my aunts and uncles were married for years. These were not perfect relationships, but they were together, and they made it work. My father and stepmother divorced after 20 years of marriage.

I envisioned that by age 30, I would be married to a loving husband, and we would have one child, a girl…maybe a small dog, no picket fence (I am not a fan of picket fences). No matter what I saw in front of me, or didn't see, I held that dream for myself in my heart. I longed to be chosen, seen, heard, protected, and loved!

I was adamant that I would wait for the special guy to come into my life. I wanted to "do life" the "right way". After all, I am a Christian. I was serious about how I carried myself as a young lady. My Christian walk was very important to me, which resulted in my being guarded as it pertains to relationships and how I communicated with young men.

I had a few crushes by the time I entered Coolidge Senior High School in the 10th grade. One of the guys graduated before I arrived, the other one was in the eleventh grade, I didn't even know his last name. The crushes faded as time passed (out of sight, out of mind). With all the class assignments and extra-curricular activities, I forgot all about them.

I had my first kiss, while walking on the way home from Paul Junior High School. It wasn't what I imagined, but it happened. We remained "just" friends after that. That was as close to "racy" as things got for me.

First Base, Second Place

Fast forward to 1989, the last quarter of my 10th Grade year...I managed to navigate my first year of high school successfully; socially and academically. Suddenly, someone was vying for my attention. He was handsome, smart, and very charismatic. The funny part is, we had been in English class together all year long, and I never looked at him "that way". He started to show me attention. I liked the attention and the compliments. For some reason, I didn't feel the need to be as guarded with him. I quickly found myself in a whirlwind of feelings and emotions that I had never allowed myself to feel and could barely articulate.

He showed an interest in me, he liked me, and that became enough. I would be neglectful if I failed to mention that I was only the "It Girl", for the moment. He had broken up with his girlfriend. I found myself negotiating not only the terms and conditions of my heart, but also my virtue. I knew right from wrong, so there was a moral war going on inside. I loved the way he made me feel, the kind words and compliments. He was giving me all of what I needed now. We'd spend hours talking on the phone learning about each other. We talked about everything, except about me being his girlfriend or conversations about the future for us. I had the purest heart and the best intentions toward him. There was nothing that I would not do for him. He had my heart. I held out hoping to be chosen, but I became part of an unhealthy dynamic. I was okay to be the "go to" friend when he wasn't with the on and off again girlfriend. This went on for about a year. **First Base, Second Place**, that was my position. This relationship was the beginning of an unhealthy pattern of not being made a priority in relationships.

I covered my hurt by smiling, while maintaining a platonic friendship with him. I was reliable and dependable, always close, but never the chosen one. He had two more relationships form and dismantle…why was I never even considered? For a year and a half, silently, I stayed on an emotional roller coaster ride. No one else could gain my attention because he had my heart. I went to the Senior Prom stag (no date), by choice. No dance, no date. I never got over it, even though it may have appeared that I did.

We reconnected just before college. I felt special, for a little while. I had not been forgotten. He went away to school. I stayed here in the city. We kept in touch by letter and phone freshman year. As time passed communication lessened. Our last telephone conversation was in the Spring of '93. Yes, I remember! We discussed what maybe could've been, if I had made the decision to come there… but I wasn't there. The question always remained in the forefront of my mind, "Why am I not enough?" "What is wrong with me?" Only I could truly answer those questions as they were rooted in low self-esteem and low self-worth. With so many tears shed, and broken hearted, I pulled what was still present of my self-esteem together and waited for the next opportunity to be seen and loved. Though the unresolved feelings and unhealed hurt remained.

The Good Guy

I found myself in a few fleeting situations, no one important enough to really note for this book. In August 1993, I met my "**Good Guy**". He was 21, I'd just turned 20. He was an engineering student at Drexel University. We met at a fraternity party. He was staying with family in the area for the summer. He was handsome, smart, and very kind to me. He was a true gentleman. When I would receive calls from him, I was always excited. We talked about everything, school, family, goals, and aspirations. To set the scene, this was before cell phones, so long-distance phone bills were a real thing. After six months, I wanted to be clear on where the relationship was going. We defined our relationship. We became a couple!

We lived two hours apart, but he made time for me, and I would make time for him. He met my family, and I met his. Sometimes when he was in town he would attend church with me, and I with him. As time passed, life and priorities changed, not only were we two hours apart in distance, but the things we wanted became very different. We started moving in dissimilar directions. Just before the Christmas holiday in 1997 I received a phone call from him. Tearfully, he stated that he was losing focus on school, and obtaining his degree, and stated that I deserved to have someone who could spend more time with me. This was the reason for our breakup after three and a half years. I did not want to let go of my relationship status. It made me feel like I belonged somewhere to someone. I didn't like the decision he made for the both of us, but I had to accept it. I cried so hard that I thought I would die in my sleep! When morning came, I realized it was not my time to go. God still had something for me to do, even though my heart was broken. I will admit, I was unhappy for quite a while because I could feel the shift in our relationship but was willing to stay in it for the sake of "being in a relationship". He accepted me just as I was, and I him. We had a mutual love and respect for one another. He was my first "official" boyfriend. What we didn't lose was friendship. He was a **Good Guy**.

I started having an internal dialogue with myself that there must be something wrong with me. I wondered if anyone else would ever take the time to get to know me. My identity was changed at my own hands. I became guarded once again and not interested in dating. I was protecting my heart from any further injury. I redirected my focus to singing, church, work, and school. I shut down my feelings for a very long time.

Gut Instinct

After three years of living my best life as a single, at 27 I was finding my own way in the workforce, working two jobs. My major focus during that time was singing with my Community Choir, PGF-VPS of Washington DC. I wasn't at all interested in dating. It was the last thing on my mind.

We were introduced by my friend who was dating his younger brother. I reluctantly held a conversation with him, still guarded, I was polite, but disinterested. After my past experiences with heartbreak, I wasn't open to the possibility of dating. A few weeks after our first brief introduction, he asked my friend if it was okay to call me. She passed on the message to me, and I agreed. As he introduced himself to me, I became less guarded. Although I was a bit concerned that he was nine years my senior and divorced with a six-year-old child. The background made me want to run, but I wanted to give him a chance, since he was coming off so nice, and wanting to get to know me.

I became enveloped in the approach I call, "The Ambassador", or what many commonly refer to as "The Representative". I was still naïve, wanting to believe the best in people. Mostly excited for the possibility of loving someone again and being loved. It was nice to have someone to call me to make sure I got home okay after a long commute, especially in the snow. I didn't know it was part of "his agenda".

We made the relationship official (or at least I did), on December 26th. This was the first day we met in person after talking on the phone for weeks. Neither of us knew what the other looked like. He had a question about whether I had a pecan tan complexion. I responded, "I guess so". We just had to wait until we met in person. I received my first cellphone for Christmas that year, and there was no video or photo component. In my heart, it didn't matter what he looked like, since he was so nice to me. Could this be the love my heart was waiting for? We were introduced in person that evening. We talked as we drove around the city, then he dropped me off at home. As I walked up the stairs, I thought to myself "He is nice, but maybe we should just be friends…", but then another thought came that I was being shallow. He wasn't my "type" aesthetically. I silenced my **Gut Instinct**. I proceeded with the relationship.

I continued to "see" him (only on occasion), but we talked every day. I'm careful not to use the term "date" because that would mean that there was some dating going on; we never went on a date. After being in a new relationship there was no honeymoon period. In less than two months, things started to take a negative turn. Red flags were swirling, I was ducking them, but I didn't stop to read them. Valentine's Day was in my rear view, it was just another day to him. I baked him chocolate chip cookies, and he didn't even bother to come to my house to get them. There were always excuses for him not coming to visit me or meet my family. That was a developing pattern.

By the end of February, after sensing tension, I asked what was going on, and he told me what was bothering him. He had a baby on the way, due in April. I was devastated. We talked about what we wanted in the future, to be married, to have a daughter and other things, but not a child by another woman! I should've followed my **Gut Instinct** and left the relationship. How do I wrap my mind around the fact that there is a woman pregnant with my boyfriend's unborn child? I struggled with this reality for the remainder of the time before she was born. His daughter was born two months later.

Months later he issued a verbal decree out of the blue that he wasn't having any more children. Not that I was planning to have a child right away, but as I stated earlier, we discussed marriage and having a child. Marriage was also taken off the table. I was devastated. I was hurt that he was not being considerate of me at all. The "official" relationship ended after 14 months. He kept me around for his "convenience" after that time. We were supposed to be maintaining a friendship, but I discovered the entire time we were "together" it was all about his "convenience". He said the breakup was because he didn't want to "do that to me!" He didn't want to be with me knowing that I wanted to be married and have children. Although he told me otherwise in the beginning of our relationship, that was no longer what he wanted. In other words, he didn't want to deprive me of my dream.

Why was I still entertaining the manipulation, and emotional abuse? I was trying to fulfill an unmet need. I stayed longer than I should've with nothing positive to show for staying with him. I never received a card or gift in all the years that I've known this man. Still not having a firm grasp of my self-worth, I lingered around waiting for him to decide if he wanted to reconsider being in a relationship with me, again. We never really stopped communicating. The experience thus far, hadn't been the best for me, but somehow, I felt validated. I was broken and unhappy, but I continued to perform and be a doormat, with no reciprocity.

What happened to the man that I met? There was little regard shown for my feelings. He was manipulative and mean. This man treated me like he was doing me a favor holding a conversation with me. It was the arrogance and the temper tantrums that caused me to spend countless days and nights in tears. I would sit and ask myself; how did I end up in a situation like this? Starving for attention. I later learned that a person can only give you love if they have love to give. Everything centered around what he needed and wanted, financially and otherwise. He was no longer the person he presented himself to be. After a year of arguing back and forth with him over a situation I found myself in that almost ended in rape. This had nothing to do with him. Instead of him being there to support me. He was very insensitive, and one day after hanging up and calling back one too many times, he made a comment that was so mean that it was finally the straw that broke the camel's back! Of all the things I could've called him, that were well deserved, I called him a jerk. His reply was as cold as liquid nitrogen. He replied, "Well since I'm a jerk, remember that friend I told you about, I married her last Friday!" He said it with such vitriol, it was evil. His words cut straight through my soul. After all I had done for him, this is how he treated me. He lied for the past year stating that this woman was just his friend. "No!" was all I could reply. I don't remember how the call ended.

A month prior he came by my house, a month prior, he called and asked me if I could bring him something to eat and a newspaper. He borrowed money from me, all a month or so before he got married. My feelings were palpable!

The embarrassment of not only being used but disrespected in such a way that my self-esteem was flat lined. I allowed this. I spent far too much time with a man who dishonored me. I demeaned myself, by staying in a relationship that never served me. All the events took such a stressful toll on my body that I ended up seriously ill. My focus turned to my undiagnosed condition. In later years he apologized, I accepted his apology. I move on.

Running On Empty

"When people show you who they are, believe them." Dr. Maya Angelou's quote rings out loud and shakes me to my core when I think about this individual. After more than a year of being angry and sulking in embarrassment after my harsh discard, I met a "male" on my daily ride to work. He presented just as he was, a hustler, a fast talker, a user! He worked around the corner from my building, so I knew he was employed, but that didn't stop him from asking me for money. I was forewarned not to get involved with him. I heard clearly in my spirit, "Don't do it." We weren't in the same place, socially, mentally, or emotionally. I wanted so badly to get emotionally unstuck from the pain, that I proceeded with giving my time and attention to a man who only set out to get whatever he could from me. He told me this later prior to our break-up. After I shared with him some of what I endured in my previous relationship, he was simply waiting his turn to receive. When I introduced him to my father, he extended his hand for a handshake and said, "What's up Pops?" Oh no…I knew it would not end well. He addressed my father as if "Pops" was his first name. My father asked me in his own special way, the next morning, who he was. He would stand me up for dates, he would leave me waiting on dates that never happened. Like a scene out of Baby Boy, he offered to detail my car. He showed up to pick me up from work promptly, the first time. After gaining my trust, the next time he didn't show up at all. I had to catch the bus home, while he drove around in my car. After a few hours and many excuses later, he stopped answering the phone. It was Good Friday. The next morning, I received a text that read "I love you". The amusing thing is he had never texted me before, ever! My reply was "If you don't have my car back in 20 minutes, I am on my way to the police precinct to report my car stolen. I did not authorize you to keep my car." I was so serious. My car was returned in less than 20 minutes, with the gas light on "E". I had never seen the gaslight warning on my dashboard. I was furious!

Once again, I allowed a man to treat me like less than a woman. Being with him was the first time that I felt like I was just an object. I can remember the moment that I felt like I had an out of body experience. I remember asking myself, "Tracy, what are you doing?"

I made up my mind from that moment on that I had enough. I couldn't believe that he once asked for all the change out of my car for beer…what was I doing? Paid on Friday, broke on Monday with no major bills, what was I doing with this person? We coasted for a few more months. I have no idea what happened between April and July. We spoke on the phone, more broken promises than I can remember. I was simply wasting time. After my birthday passed and he didn't call or text to wish me a happy birthday, I waited to see just how creative his excuse would be this time. He told me that so many people in his family have birthdays in July…I tuned out the remainder of the conversation he was "shoveling". He told me that he was going to a cookout that evening. I said nothing. After thinking about all that had transpired in the past four and a half months.

I decided that I was no longer going to participate in the foolishness. I had enough. I left him a voicemail message on his cell phone, that I no longer wanted to continue the relationship. I had no hard feelings, but I was done. I received no reply to my message. The next day, I followed up with a text message to ensure he got the message. Believe it or not, that "male" called me on Monday evening, three days later! I answered the phone and the first thing he asked was "You fired me?" I said yes! He said, "That's okay, you're still my baby though." I got off the phone. That was indeed a "good" good-bye. No looking back. I was "delete the telephone number" done! A month or so later, he called and asked to "borrow" money. That was an easy no for me. I had regrets about not being obedient to the Holy Spirit in the beginning, but I never looked back.

Unfinished Business

Hope deferred maketh the heart sick: but when the desire cometh, it is a tree of life. (Proverbs 13:12, KJV). I "saw" him, and he "saw" me! We were introduced by a mutual acquaintance. After all I had experienced in previous relationships, I was guarded, and my self-esteem and ego were on the floor.

He was strikingly handsome, tall, and bronzed with the most beautiful smile, and his caring eyes drew me in. We didn't talk very much in the beginning, a smile, and a wave with a brief word or two at first. He was a gentleman, very respectful and complementary. I was still suffering through symptoms of connective tissue disease, which made me feel even more self-conscious. He seemed shy, but very friendly. We lost touch for a while, then our paths crossed a few months later. I was so happy to see him because I would think about him from time to time.

He took an interest in me, who I was, how I felt. He was a great listener. It felt too good to be true to meet a man so consistently kind. I knew I was in a fragile place emotionally, but with him, I easily let my guard down. I felt safe. He made me feel very special. A loving friendship developed. He needed me as much as I needed him. We would hold what we called "therapy sessions". He was there for me, and I for him. We built a true friendship. We encouraged each other. I felt as if he was my biggest cheerleader, and I was always "riding" for him. As time progressed, he helped to rebuild my confidence.

The relationship status became less defined as strictly platonic as the years passed, because we blurred the line between platonic friendship and love.

We began to speak two different languages. We were bi-lingual! There were platonic feelings of genuine care most of the time, but it got complicated when feelings grew stronger over time. Years passed and I held on to the possibility of there being more between us.

I was as open and honest as I could be about every aspect of my life. He was not as open. He started speaking a language that I could no longer understand. After everything we had gone through together, I couldn't wrap my mind around what was happening. In the end, I didn't like what he told me. It defied all logical sense. One of the things I didn't do was ask certain questions in the beginning like, "Are you married, or in a relationship"? It would've been difficult to discuss, but I wouldn't have felt like I was hit, blindsided. I was there for him through a rough situation. We were intimate (in the truest sense of the word). A woman's intuition is one of her greatest gifts, mine felt like a curse to me. Not only was there "the other" situation he had to work through, but I later learned he was seeing someone romantically. He chose someone else!

Here I go again… I tried to love him to the best of my ability. My little girl recognized the wounded little boy in him. Sometimes when we love, we have to not hold on, but let go. He was my "Ace", I was his "Quan". This was difficult!

I felt abandoned, again. He promised he would always be there for me; but it was no longer possible in the way that I needed. I had to learn to love him differently, and from a distance. I continue to pray for him daily. I was forced to refocus and redirect that love I gave back to myself, or I wouldn't make it. There will always remain things left undone, and words left unspoken–unfinished business. In the meantime, I pray to God to grant me peace, over the situation, and a forgiving heart for him and myself. I am now more in-tune and honest with my feelings. Healing is taking place in my heart.

<u>In the 21 days, I had many reflections and takeaways</u>:

- To get a different result, I must do something different!
- You don't get over the pain, you must go through the pain.
- The work that I'm doing isn't only for me, but to reach back and pull someone else through their pain.

When I feel emotionally heavy, I know it is okay to cry! One morning in particular, I felt the tears coming, I just let them fall: without shame. I used to cry and hurry up and wipe my tears quickly. I would cry in the shower, because the water and my tears mixed well, and no one could hear me as the tears ran down the drain. No one had to know. This time, after I cried, I got up and pressed on with my day, with no embarrassment. My beautifully wounded soul was healing. I now embrace my tears as a part of my healing. It was cathartic. I thanked the Lord for the healing that was taking place. Suppressing my emotions has been counterproductive to my healing. God gave us tears, it's okay to express your feelings. The longer you suppress pain, the further delayed the healing process. Sometimes the tears are cute, streaming down your face, and sometimes you may have to let out "the ugly cry", just remember it's okay!

The 21 days allowed me to reflect on each of my past relationships. I still have a great deal of "heart-work" ahead of me. Processing and healing from the abandonment and rejection feelings are going to take more work, but this process was a start in the right direction. I am clear that I'm not a victim! I have a choice in every situation. I choose to take my power back! I won't leave my healing to someone else. My healing is my responsibility! I challenge anyone reading this book to make the choice to take your power back and not succumb to heartbreak. Heartbreak is a normal part of life. Learn from the experiences and adopt a different perspective. You can live forward in a positive way.

I have given my love, honor, and respect in relationships, this includes family and platonic relationships, not just romantic relationships. Some didn't acknowledge or appreciate my efforts. I have many long-lasting friendships that have withstood the test of time, but I've had a few disappointing ends to some friendships. I have even felt betrayal at the hands of a close friend. I believe in "the code". Here is a snapshot of the situation. I had a crush on a guy that

I knew for quite a while, we had mutual friends in common and would socialize often in close quarters. When I found out that he liked me, I was flattered, but I could not pursue anything with him because I was in a relationship with **The Good Guy**. Well, my friend dishonored "the code". She knew that I liked him a lot and he liked me, but the timing was not good because I was already committed. She had a one-time fling (they had relations without the "ship"). It was the nonchalant attitude that hurt me more than anything. She was my friend, she knew me. Of all the men in the DC Metropolitan area, why him? I was not only hurt, but disappointed.

We weren't the same after that, I loved her like my own sister, and felt such disregard for my feelings. Life goes on and time has passed, I've forgiven her. I don't want to hold her to what happened over 20 years ago. I've made peace with my decision to allow people to leave my life. I'm no longer holding on to relationships that need to end. I've made a huge error in the past of putting others' feelings ahead of my own and staying in relationships that didn't serve me longer than I needed to stay. My feelings matter! I deserve to be loved, honored, and respected in all relationships. After counseling and coaching I'm very clear about my boundaries and won't accept treatment from anyone who dishonors me.

We live in a reality television and social media society. We see relationships flaunted daily! As a hopeless romantic, it's totally okay for me to celebrate the love that I see others display, and equally okay to take a break from seeing the posts of the "good stuff" people want you to see on social media. Sometimes I need a break from all the stories. It's not a jealousy thing per se, but I don't want to romanticize situations that I see in a one-dimensional view. We only see what's being shared when there's often more to a story. I know when I need to keep my eyes focused forward. Jealousy and comparison are a thief of peace and joy. I believe wholeheartedly that what God has for me, is just for me!

The outcome of my past relationships doesn't determine my value! In some cases, I casted my pearls to swine (Matthew 7:6, KJV). Therefore, I take responsibility for my tolerance of the mistreatment. Today is a new day. I'm no longer looking back in regret, I look back to examine the patterns, and to determine the lessons. I am the star of my life's story, the most important person in my life! My needs and feelings matter. I prioritize my needs and wants first. I will no longer waste energy in situations that don't serve me or make me a better person.

I now realize that I am the prize! A prize never chases down the recipient of the gift. For that reason, I will no longer chase after anyone in pursuit of love. I must admit that I have put on the full court press in some of my past relationships. I spent way too much time to win attention. As the saying goes, "When you know better, you do better". Despite it all, I'm sure there are a few guys in my past who will one day acknowledge me as "the one that got away!"

In reflecting on many of my experiences, I realize that if I hadn't processed the disappointment, the trauma, the lessons, and heartache I experienced, I may not have discovered who Tracy Monique truly is, and what I'm made of. Sometimes the pain inflicted upon us is intentional. Sometimes we become collateral damage as others are living out their pain. Either way, pain is pain. I'm a true believer that hurt people, hurt people! I consider myself "functionally heartbroken". This is truly a process, but I'm being kind to myself as I move through the process. I keep growing, glowing, and showing up…but on the inside there's still brokenness, sadness and sometimes anger.

After intense coaching and counseling, instead of looking at these relationships as things that happened to me, I now see them as things that happened for me. I was hiding what I needed God to heal. I'm clear about what I need and want and will no longer compromise.

I'm working on myself to be all that I expect of my partner, physically and emotionally.

I always wanted to escape the aftermath of feelings of pain and disappointment that follow the ending of a relationship. I wanted to wake up and have it one day pass over me. I was hoping that time would heal my wounding, even though I didn't want to do the work required! I've learned to embrace the pain, sit in it, and feel it–facing it head on. I've suffered through the torment of disregarded feelings, not being chosen, being taken advantage of, and dishonored. I had to surrender it all! I mean not just say it, or sing it, but truly surrender it all to God. I have no desire to seek revenge or rehearse retaliation. My focus is on my present and future. I pray daily for God to heal my heart, my mind, and my emotions. This is an ongoing work in progress.

I invest more time into finding out how to love myself better. I had been existing and not living. I'm no longer waiting for "Prince Charming" to come into my life in order to start living. Today, I choose to live out loud, on purpose.

CHAPTER 4

The Actual 21 Day No Contact Challenge Process

This was an incredibly difficult process; however, it was also necessary. With every challenge there will always be people who commit to doing something, but they don't fully engage for one reason or another. I had to remind myself not to get upset by the lack of commitment to the process, especially since this was more of an individual process than collective. When we started it was asked and agreed upon that everyone follow ALL the rules as they were explained. Two of us did and two of us didn't. I think that the effort of each lady was good, but when all the individuals in the collective or group don't complete each of the basic activities: daily prayer call, journaling, watching recommended videos by relationship gurus, the process' maximum results may not be achieved. A portion of us doing the activities and following the ground rules was also created so that we could give input on what everyone else was sharing during the daily video calls. This process literally took at least 21 days of concentration, focus, and commitment to the process regardless of what was taking place in our lives. Life brought some obstacles and challenges for sure during that time! Pushing past it all is what allowed us to reach the goals we initially wanted and far beyond that!

Learning to sit in our feelings and praying to God instead of calling each other when we had those rough days was also important. Maybe, even more so. For this reason, if I did this process again with a different group of females or were to instruct others about this process, I would not give out each other's contact numbers until the end. I would schedule the Google Meet, but if we didn't have each other's numbers until after the 21 days ended then there may have been less temptation to call each other on those difficult days. Instead, we'd talk to God first in prayer especially since we wouldn't always be available to speak to each other. However, God is always available to hear and listen to what is on our heart. Sometimes when we have other people in our ears, it can cause us not to hear God's voice and that is not a place I, nor Tracy ever wants to be again!

Seeing that the only person we could speak to about this process was our therapist, and only one of us went consistently, one went once, two made an appointment and did not hear back from the therapist. It would've been even more beneficial to have a therapist to help us process. I must be honest I was disappointed when everyone wasn't able to have at least one counseling session over the three weeks,

I'm honored that God would choose these ladies and me (Lisa) to go on this journey regardless of our pasts. I pray that our experiences will help others make better decisions, live joyful lives, and prosper, as their souls prosper (3 John 1:2, KJV).

CHAPTER 5

Proceed with Caution...Maintenance is Necessary! Blog written by Lisa Louise GIlliam

While writing this book, I began to realize that most of my relationships, friendships included, were lopsided. I began to see that I was treated badly or used in many of my relationships-familial, platonic friendships, and romantic relationships. There was little to no maintenance and maintenance was definitely necessary.

When building something you must first have a foundation, preferably a strong one. Most people want whatever they're building to be crafted with specific details, but unless you have the money to do that, it may or may not be constructed the way you planned it. Nonetheless, if you put in the time, save the money necessary, etc., you may not only be able to purchase the materials you desire for what you're building, but also purchase the best quality materials.

As with many things the quality of the material may determine how long it will last, which can, in return, reduce the amount of maintenance necessary in the long run. This is because nothing lasts forever! You have to put work into it. In essence, some sort of maintenance, repair, and if you're not careful, replacement, restoration, etc., will take place at some point over the years. Sometimes when we realize whatever we have built needs work, we decide to prolong the maintenance which can become a costly repair or irreparable damage. Then we think back on how things might have been if we had been proactive when we first found out there was a problem. We ask ourselves things like, "We had the money, so why did we procrastinate and not take care of the problem immediately?" Or maybe your question is, "Why didn't we save the money all along, because we know repairs may be needed eventually?" "Why didn't we put the time in or hire someone for regular check-ups knowing this may have saved us costly repairs or replacements in the future?" It almost always costs less to repair than it does to replace!

Just like we need a strong foundation when we are building physical things, we also need the same when it comes to building friendships! Friendship is a two-sided, give and take relationship. There will be ups and downs. Since no relationship is without conflicts, I believe that when there are problems they should be resolved before jumping to conclusions or ending the relationship. So many things can be clarified if the time is taken to communicate. I'm grateful for those people who are dependable and show through their actions that our friendship means something to them. But honestly, there came a time in my life that I began to have a lot of questions about some of my friendships. Maybe it's me…maybe it isn't, but I'm doing more self-checks to find out! My prayer is that once I'm finished with this self-check that I will have a better understanding of my role in the friendships I've developed. I also hope to have a better understanding of the people in my life who are genuine, and those who aren't. Nevertheless, I've been learning a lot about me, my friendships and setting boundaries. I do have God. He has blessed me with some awesome friends and acquaintances to be able to reach out to. One day I was driving home from work thinking about the many relationships I've gained and lost over the years. There are certain people I truly miss, while others, I'm glad we're no longer in a relationship. Now, many people think of relationships with regards to "love" relationships, but here I'm speaking about family relationships and friendships as well. In my opinion we all should learn to build relationships on a strong foundation. Principles, values, faith, are all parts of that. Then many of us have specific details that we desire as well. These qualities are priceless and important to us individually. They could consist of being funny, tall, short, sports lover, or other characteristics and commonalities. By spending quality time with the person, we find out if they have the qualities we desire. As the relationship grows, you will notice that maintenance is also needed. If you don't find out and deal with the things that can or are causing issues in your relationship (any relationship) or continue to fine tune the things that are going right, there may be damage and repair is needed. When this is the case, make sure you communicate. If you must, use counseling or a restorative conversation as a way to strengthen or repair what has been broken. If this relationship, friendship, or otherwise, is important to you, spend the time you need to work on the bond and with just as much care as you did when you first built it. If this isn't done, it can cause you to lose what you formed. Why put the time into building something if you aren't going to maintain it? All relationships, whether it is family, friendships, or "love "relationships should be established on a solid foundation and maintained in order to operate in its fullest capacity! Thus, proceed with caution and do the maintenance required to keep the relationship working effectively, because if you don't, you'll end up with just a "ship" and no relations.

CHAPTER 6

Define The Relationship, Ask Questions

Tracy and I didn't decide to share our stories because we're proud of our actions or situations. However, we decided to share our stories, so others won't make the same mistakes we've made. How can you avoid some of the pitfalls that we had? First pray and listen to God! He knows far better than you do what is best for you. Next, define the relationship. Contrary to popular belief, it's alright to ask the person what they want with regards to the two of you dating. Ask the question, what are you looking for in a relationship? If you find yourself wanting a relationship and the other person doesn't, please don't put all of your eggs into one basket. Instead, date, have fun and take the time to get to know each other. Then, once you've defined the relationship and decide to date exclusively (court), think about what type of marriage you'd like. Be willing to ask the difficult but real questions such as:

Relationships

- Do you believe in a monogamous relationship?
- Are you married or have you ever been married?
- Do you still have romantic ties to an ex?
- When was your last relationship and are you ready to start a new one with me?
- Have you ever cheated or been cheated on while in a relationship?
- Have you been proposed to or proposed to someone before?
- Have you been engaged, married, or divorced previously?
- Do you believe in living together before marriage?
- Do you believe in divorce?
- What is your love language?
- Do you want to know details about all of my past relationships, serious or otherwise?
- Are you willing to participate in a weekly date night? When? What happens if one of you must cancel? Do you reschedule immediately or let time pass until the next scheduled date night?
- If I'm platonic friends with someone I used to date, or was in a relationship with are you ok with that? Can we still go out for coffee or a meal? If so, are any of these off limits?
- Are you open to having a ladies' night or men's night out? What about a weekend where your significant other/spouse goes away for a weekend with their friends? Do they have to be of the same sex?
- How do you identify yourself (gender, sexual orientation, etc.)? What is your dating preference?

Lisa L. Gilliam and Tracy M. Worley

NOTES:

_____

_____

_____

_____

_____

_____

_____

_____

_____

_____

_____

_____

_____

_____

_____

_____

_____

_____

_____

_____

Moral Beliefs

- What are your moral beliefs and interests?
- What religion do you believe in?
- What, if any, church do you attend?
- Is it important for us to attend the same church?
- Is it important for us to attend church weekly?
- Does it matter what day of the week we attend the service?

NOTES:

_____

_____

_____

_____

_____

_____

_____

_____

_____

_____

_____

_____

_____

_____

_____

Family Matters

- Do you have children or want children? If so, how many? How soon?

- Do we raise our children in the same religion?

- What if one person's physical health prohibits pregnancy? What are your feelings and thoughts around that topic? How do you feel about adoption, becoming a foster parent or surrogacy?

- Have you ever had sex with or been in a relationship with someone of the same sex? How many times? How long ago? Are you interested in doing that again? How does each person feel about that?

NOTES:

_____

_____

_____

_____

_____

_____

_____

_____

_____

_____

_____

_____

Physical and Mental Health

- Have you ever had any sexually transmitted infections? What kind? When or how long ago?

- Do you get tested for HIV and other sexually transmitted infections? How often?

- How do you feel about going to the doctor on at least an annual basis for a review of your physical health?

- If either of you gain or lose weight in the relationship is that a deal breaker for you?

- How important is it that your significant other/spouse maintain the same physical appearance they had when you first met for the duration of the relationship? Is this a realistic expectation?

- How do you feel about counseling and therapy? Will you support, participate and/or attend therapy sessions if asked to attend?

- Do you believe in getting vaccinations (COVID-19, influenza, pneumonia, etc.)?

- Do you go to the dentist twice a year for your bi-annual dental exams?

NOTES:

_____

_____

_____

_____

_____

_____

Finances/Legal Concerns

- Do you believe in tithing (giving 10% of your gross income earned monthly) to a church?

- Do you believe in the importance of saving money? How much should we save?

- Do we decide to make big purchases together or on a whim?

- After marriage, should we have the same bank account, separate bank accounts, or both?

- How do we pay the bills?

- Do we have a family budget or an individual budget?

- Does each person have access and knowledge to all of each other's financial accounts?

- Do you believe in giving financially to charitable causes? If so, how much?

- Do you believe in having a prenuptial agreement?

- Do you believe in purchasing identity theft protection?

- Are you up to date on filing your taxes?

NOTES:

_____

_____

_____

_____

_____

_____

_____

Caregiving

- Are you a caregiver or responsible for assisting family members financially, taking them to doctor appointments, etc.?

- What happens if our parents can no longer live in the home by themselves? Do they move in with us or do we find care elsewhere?

NOTES:

_____

_____

_____

_____

_____

_____

_____

_____

_____

_____

_____

_____

_____

_____

_____

Communication

- What type of communicator are you? Do you withdraw, confront, avoid, etc.?
- How well do you communicate (listening and expressing your feelings)?
- How do you best communicate (talking through a matter, or in writing (not texting)?
- Do we agree to never go to bed angry after an argument?

NOTES:

_____

_____

_____

_____

_____

_____

_____

_____

_____

_____

_____

_____

_____

_____

Social Media

- Do we follow each other on social media?

- Do you announce that you are in a relationship on social media and tag each other's names?

- Can your significant other join certain groups and engage with people of the opposite sex on social media?

- Is speaking to someone of the opposite sex in a direct message considered cheating for you?

NOTES:

_____

_____

_____

_____

_____

_____

_____

_____

_____

_____

_____

_____

_____

_____

Employment

- If one of us loses our job, is there an expectation to get another job immediately?

- Do you have any salary expectations for each other entering the marriage?

- Who will purchase the employee offered benefits such as health insurance, life insurance, etc. for us, the family?

NOTES:

_____

_____

_____

_____

_____

_____

_____

_____

_____

_____

_____

_____

_____

_____

Household

- Do we purchase a new home or move into a residence neither of us have lived in previously or move into a place where one of us already lives?
- If one of us moves into a property that the other is purchasing or has purchased, do we put the newly married individual in the deed?
- Who will be responsible for cooking, cleaning, vacuuming the house?
- Do you wash clothes for each other, just yourself, the children?
- Do we iron and wash our own clothes?
- Who goes to the grocery store? Will it be done together or individually and whose money do we use to purchase the food?

NOTES:

_____

_____

_____

_____

_____

_____

_____

_____

_____

_____

_____

These are not the only questions that you may want to ask each other when deciding to move forward in the relationship. These are just a few of the questions that we think are worth discussing. With that being said, we do believe that YOU are worth taking this challenge. It can change the rest of your life. Take the plunge and then leave a comment on my website's page www.LisaLGilliam.com to let me know how this book or the 21 Days No Contact Challenge has positively impacted you, too.

Lisa L. Gilliam (1SingingLady)

(FoCal Grae Images by Calvin Gray)

Lisa L. Gilliam (1SingingLady) has been singing and writing since the age of 7. She has a Bachelor of Arts degree in Speech and Drama with a minor in vocal music performance from Virginia Union University (VUU). Lisa also holds a Master of Arts degree in Education and Human Development with a concentration in Community Counseling from The George Washington University (GW).

Professionally, Lisa is known for the manner in which she integrates her training and experience as a former counselor and educator with her artistic talents especially at conferences, seminars and workshops. Lisa is the founder of The Stigma Breakers' Collective (TSBC), a group of like-minded individuals, businesses, and/or organizations that also seek to break the stigmas often associated with mental health. In addition to being a mental health advocate, Lisa is also a restorative practices practitioner, speaker, vocalist, writer, spoken-word artist and poet that is intentional about integrating mental health awareness with the performance, communication, and literary arts. Therefore, whether Lisa is singing, reciting poetry/spoken word, acting or speaking/presenting at a conference, seminar, or workshop, she wants her words to be melodic...like music to your ears!

To book Lisa for your event visit www.LisaLGilliam.com. Listen to her LLG's #RandomButReal Podcast on Spotify and Anchor.FM, subscribe and watch encouraging messages and live performances on her YouTube channel www.Youtube.com/OneSingingLady, and follow her on Facebook, Instagram, TikTok, and Twitter @1SingingLady.

You may also listen to Lisa's original songs and spoken-word cd's, Past to Present (2004), God Delivered Me (single) (2015), and Depend (2019) digitally via her website, Amazon Music, Apple Music, Spotify, Tidal, or anywhere music can be downloaded or streamed.

Tracy M. Worley

(FoCal Grae Images by Calvin Gray)

Tracy Monique Worley is a native Washingtonian. A gifted orator and writer since an early age, Tracy uses her gifts to uplift, educate and entertain.

She is a career Fed, and a Self-Care and Wellness Entrepreneur. A natural creative, Tracy has many other unlisted talents. A Diamond Life member of Delta Sigma Theta Sorority, Inc. Service to the Community is a high priority.

She received a full academic scholarship from The DC School Club and holds a BA with honors from the University of the District of Columbia in Public Health Education, and an AA in Child Development.

She is a member of Gethsemane Baptist Church, Washington, DC.

Her personal motto is: Live life and leave a legacy!

Tracy is currently in the process of writing her novel, "Chosen".

www.bytracym.com

CPSIA information can be obtained
at www.ICGtesting.com
Printed in the USA
BVHW011817101122
651682BV00010B/283